HOW TO ATTRACT TRAFFIC TO YOUR WEBSITE

... and Make Money

N. K. Brooks

Legal Note: The author of this book has used her knowledge and efforts with the objective of collecting the information appeared in this publication. The information contained in this book has character purely educative; in this sense, if the reader wishes to apply some of the ideas exposed in this book, it will be under his or her own responsibility. The author, in any case, is not held responsible for any direct or indirect damage derived from the use (or misuse) of this book. The information included in this publication is offered in good faith and believing to be exact at the moment of its publication, being subjected to any necessary modifications. This book is not intended for use as a source of legal, business, accounting or financial advice. All readers are advised to seek services of competent professionals in legal, business, accounting and finance fields.

Cover Image:

Search Engines. Author: FindYourSearch/flickr.com

Table of Content

Chapter 1: Introduction 4

Chapter 2: Setting Up a Website 9

Chapter 3: Designing Your Website 17

Chapter 4: Uploading a Website 18

Chapter 5: Optimizing Your Webpage 22

Chapter 6: Link Building for Success 29

Chapter 7: Writing Articles 35

Chapter 8: Newsletters & Ezines 41

Chapter 9: Forums 45

Chapter 10: Syndicate Your Business 48

Chapter 11: Press Releases 50

Chapter 12: Social Bookmarking Sites 52

Chapter 13: Create a Blog 57

Chapter 14: Ping Services 60

Chapter 15: Viral Marketing 63

Chapter 16: Pay per Click (PPC) 64

Chapter 17: Cost per Action Advertising 67

Chapter 18: Buying Publicity Space 68

Chapter 19: Incentive Marketing 69

Chapter 20: Buying Online Traffic 70

Chapter 21: Affiliate Marketing 71

Chapter 22: Social Networking 74

Chapter 23: Mailing Lists 76

Chapter 24: Off-line Marketing 78

Chapter 25: Other Ways of Generating Traffic 80

Chapter 26: Check Results 90

Chapter 27: Conclusion 92

Index of Illustrations 96

Chapter 1: Introduction

Do not have any doubt about it, the Internet is the future! At the moment, we use just a small fraction of the potential of the World Wide Web, but in the near future more and more businesses and organization will heavily rely on the Internet while our entire environments will be focused on new technologies.

Despite all of the technological development, the basis of the global economy is still the same – buying and selling. Nonetheless, the dynamics of marketing online is very different from traditional marketing. Traffic is the key to success on Internet, as there is a fortune to be made online but must people just do not how to do it. There are a number of tricks and techniques that will help you to attract hundreds or even thousands of visitors to your websites on a weekly basis.

If you want to become an online marketer, it is crucial to remember that competition is furious and, therefore, you need to have an extra edge to make your business or website stand out amongst the millions out there.

When joining the fascinating online world, you will need a website. A website is like the business card of an online business, a window through which people look in and search for information, products, or services. These visitors are known as traffic, which is a good indicator of the site's popularity.

Traffic will also have a say when other webmasters have to consider your advertising proposals. Through traffic webmasters can also check which pages are more popular and which are less visited. This data can further help them to determine trends on the site, and tailor their offers accordingly.

What we need to remember when marketing on the Internet is that users are a community and they will trust their fellow online users.

Therefore, building a reputation in forums, chats, and blogs will make a difference in the marketing world.

Communications within Internet marketing is like the "word of mouth" of the World Wide Web. It is essential to use social networking platforms like Facebook, Twitter, or

MySpace, as they allow the users to chat, message, video chat, voice chat, share files and links, write blogs, and join discussion boards.

Social networks are, therefore, likely to become a key resource for all kinds of businesses, enable small businesses to obtain a contact base and identify their target market while obtaining future clients.

Besides social networks, social bookmarking will also help you to get visibility and attract traffic to your website, as it allows your website to be indexed and more likely to be accessed by fellow Internet users.

Offering a good service or creating a good product is just a small part of the adventure. You will soon learn that it does not matter how good your product or service is, if you actually are unable to market it appropriately.

When realizing that traffic is the key of success, most people feel overwhelmed by the idea of having to invest a huge amount of money to pay for traditional methods of traffic generation and the time that it implies. Nonetheless, there are methods to generate traffic for FREE.

When newcomers to Internet Marketing first get involved in the entire process of creating their own products, designing sales, or landing pages and trying to gain enough traffic to make sales, they often get lost. Losing your way in the Internet wasteland will push you towards throwing in the towel before time, while not understanding the options available to you for generating a traffic flow will result in few, if any, sales.

This eBook has been created bearing in mind the needs of the newcomers in Internet Marketing and it is focused on how to generate FREE traffic with any or all of the successful techniques presented here. Just one piece of advice, do not try to master all methods at once as you will not have enough time to do so and will make lots of mistakes in the process. Instead, try to master one method at a time for better results.

Chapter 2: Setting Up a Website

The first step to start generating traffic is to set up a useful website, very easy to access and navigate for visitors.

The good news is that there are several options for building a website. You can create it yourself using HTML coding, a word processor, an HTML editor, or the easiest of them, blogs like WordPress. If you use a word processor or an HTML editor, you can create a site using a template or the tools within these programs.

HTML Coding

HTML is a programming language used for building websites, which is generally easier to learn than other programming languages as everything is conveyed through a series of tags and attributes.

HTML is easy enough to learn through a book or an online tutorial. However, if you want to create more powerful websites, you will want to learn how to use scripting languages in conjunction with HTML.

Word Processor

Most modern-day word processing software such as Microsoft Word or Word Perfect can create HTML documents. You would design the webpage as you would any other document except you would save it as HTML, a web page, or any other similar option given by your word processor.

Depending upon how recent your word processing program is, you might even be able to design your website using a 'web layout' view. This view is more reflective of how your web page would look in a browser, making it a better choice when creating your website.

The negative side is that websites created with word processors tend to display oddly, being really difficult to fix everything properly and it becoming necessary to invest hours and hours of editing to obtain a more or less decent result.

In this case, the only option out there is trying to keep the website as simplest as possible. Consider this, it is better to have a short but nice website that still fulfils the objective of making money than a large and unprofessional site that could discredit yourself and your product.

HTML Editor

HTML editor programs are designed to help you create or edit HTML, without having previous knowledge of HTML.

The most famous and used HTML editors are Dreamweaver and Microsoft Office FrontPage. They are more expensive than word processors (except FrontPage), but the final result is more accurate.

Templates

Website templates can be used in word processor and with HTML editors being an alternative for those who do not have the time and/or knowledge necessary to design the graphical elements of a website.

There are literally thousands of free templates available and equally effective than a paid one but with simpler designs. You can also find affordable templates on sites like www.e-Bay.com.

Another alternative is using templates from your web hosting company, as usually these templates can be used through a separate editor from within your web hosting account. You can also find web-hosting companies like Yahoo Stores, which are specialized in the creation of online stores, allowing you to build an e-commerce site similar to the ones of Amazon.com or Buy.com.

Blog Templates

Another possibility of building a website is to use templates created for blogs, being WordPress the best option. WordPress is probably the most popular software to set up blogs, as it has some good advantages like the fact that it is free of charge while it offers a great number of gidgets, which are very easy to set and use and are able to transform your page into a highly professional website. Additionally, WordPress does not require any technical or computing knowledge, as everyone can set his/her own website just by following a few simple step described in the blog.

Using WordPress is simple although, of course, at the beginning everybody makes mistakes and you could feel a little bit overwhelmed until you know the page.

WordPress offers tutorials, online help, and forums where users can ask questions and obtain information. You can also find tutorials n how to use WordPress in the video sharing platform YouTube.

WordPress has the advantage over the previous options because it is very easy to use, offers a great variety of designs, and it is highly effective at the moment of attracting traffic.

Besides, WordPress offers the possibility of creating a blog that looks like a website. If you do not wish to have your visitors come across a WordPress address, as it could not be professional enough, you can buy a domain and connect it with WordPress.

In this way you could work with WordPress but the domain that your visitors will come across when accessing your page will not be a blog but that domain that you have chosen and purchased.

To do this, you will have to acquire a domain and online space, a point that will be explained in deep in the next chapters.

Hiring the Services of a Designer

If the idea of building a website looks too complicated to you or you do not have enough time to dedicate to this task, think about hiring the services of a professional web designer.

There are some good websites where you could find freelance web designers and writers like www.elance.com, www.fiverr.com or www.getafreelancer.com.

At the moment of hiring the services of a designer, it is indispensable that you carefully read the reviews of other users and require the final price for the service, examples of previous projects, and, if possible, professional references.

Pre-Design Pages

Another option is to purchase a pre-made website through platforms like www.ebay.com.

These pages basically are ready-made sites with the graphical layout and the content developed and you only have to upload your website to a hosting website account, introduce the content, and start the marketing campaign of your site.

Chapter 3: Designing Your Website

The first thing to bear in mind when it comes down to website design is keep your layout simple. Most effective websites have their logo and banner advertising on the top, links to other websites on the left side, and content on the right side or links on both the left and right sides with the content in the middle.

Be careful with the colors and the layouts, combining soft colors that do not cause headaches or refusal to visitors and inserting easy and simple layouts that allow people to find the information that they are looking for without getting lost in the pages or spending several minutes wandering around. Therefore, create eye-catching and descriptive titles and structure your content in such a way that invites people to read. Also, use multi-media content that offers a fun experience to visitors.

Chapter 4: Uploading a Website

In order to upload your site on the Internet you will need web hosting, at least you can use WordPress and buy a domain name, which is the address that visitor's type when entering your site. Web hosting can be free (you will be required to place their advertising on your website in exchange for the price of the web hosting while their look is limited regarding designs) or paid, which, in general, look more professional.

There are some providers that offer both things: domain and spaces. Nevertheless, it is not obligatory to buy both services from the same provider. So, if you find a website that offers cheap domains, you can purchase your domain on that page and then buy the space from another.

At the moment of purchasing a domain, you will have to do a little research that helps you choose the perfect name for your site.

If you wish to attract traffic, it is essential that your site domain contain, what in online marketing is called, SEO keywords. These keywords are words that user look for more often when developing an online search.

In doing so, you can use a free service offered by Google called Google Trends, in which you can introduce one or several words that will let you know what are the most popular searches.

The best is to elaborate a list with possible names for your website and then introduce those words in Google Trends in order to know which are the most popular searches and use that word or that combination of words in the name of your website.

Another tip to generate traffic to your website is to choose, always if it is possible, a .com domain.

Concerning web hosting, there are pages that offer this service at a very good price.

It is recommended that this site offer access to a cPanel, which is a program that automatically connects your domain and space to WordPress without the need of developing a HTML program. This means that, once you have acquired your domain and space, the provider will give you a code to enter in your cPanel, which will play the role of linking with WordPress. In this way, you can build your website using WordPress, which will be much easier and cheaper but showing your chosen domain to your visitor, giving a more professional appearance. This page also offers cheap domain and packages, which include one or several email addresses.

A cheap alternative is using a URL redirect service such as www.namestick.com or www.stablehost.com. With a URL redirect service, you buy a domain name that will 'replace' your old domain name, at least to the eyes of your visitors. These pages are economic and come with a good client service.

If you do not have computer knowledge it is essential that you acquire hosting space in a site that offers you the chance of working from a cPanel, as you will not find an easier and faster way to develop your site.

A good piece of advice is to ask friends and relative for their honest opinion on your website before you focus your efforts on attracting traffic. -Once your website is perfectly set up, it is time to generate traffic.

Chapter 5: Optimizing Your Webpage

The first step towards success in the world of Internet Marketing is to increase your page visibility, this means to be able to place your site in a really good ranking position.

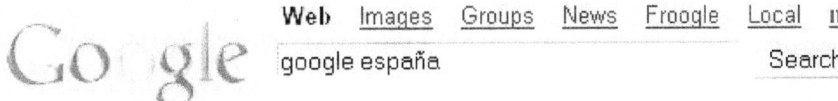

This means that when you search for a website through a search engine like Google (you should work preferably with Google it is by far the most demanded search engine) the results obtained after a search that is the ranking. If you site is located in the first or second page of the results displayed, you are doing your job properly.

Bear in mind that when people look for something on the Internet, they invariably will have a look at the first results displayed by the search engine. So, it is crucial that your website be located in the first positions.

There are a number of tips to obtain this goal. One is to have Google material on your website, links to YouTube, a Gmail address, a Google map of your business and a profile on Google+.

The reason to use Google material is that Google is the most powerful and used search engine and it has a tendency to give preference to those pages that use its free services.

Once you have all your Google material, focus your efforts on generating traffic. In doing so, you should improve your SEO words and optimize it continuously.

Optimizing your Website

The search engines have software programs called crawlers, or spiders, which are able to detect keywords and labels in the pages and generate a ranking of results based on the collected information.

At the moment of optimizing your website you should learn to use adequately the keywords or SEO.

Keywords or SEO (Search Engine Optimization) words are those words that are more likely to be searched by Internet users and should be included in any text, from articles to news passing from websites.

In doing so, you should use a keyword analyzer such as Word Tracker (paid), Yahoo Overture Keyword Selector Tool (free), or Google Trends (free) to have a picture of the words more searched through the search engine. Just go to the site and enter in a search term and the program will offer a result that will allow you to know if a word is being searched by users or not.

These keywords have to be included in every title and headline, in the description of every image included in the website, in the description of your page in your HTML code, in the tags of your source code, in the first two sentences of each paragraph, and throughout the text in the same way of a spider web.

A good technique to obtain keywords is to analyze the topic that you are going to write about and elaborate a list with those works that you believe the users will search for in order to find the information contained in your text. Then, visit one of the keywords analysis tool already mentioned and check the popularity of those words. The tool will offer you alternatives, improving your keywords.

The general guideline for creating web content is to write a list of keywords to include in a text and make sure your keyword density is 2 to 6 percent. For instance, if you have content of 500 words, your keyword should be included 10 to 30 times, mainly in headlines and titles while distributing them in a way like that of a spider web throughout the text and being careful of not overdoing it or your site might get flagged for spam while your text will lose quality.

If you use WordPress, you can add in just a few clicks, a plugin called WordPress SEO, which will analyze each post published, offering you a complete analysis on percentages and giving you tips to optimize the post.

A good SEO plan will generate better return on your investment than most other plans. Therefore, it is crucial to choose the keywords properly finding a balance between highly competitive keywords and those that are not so popular or competitive but still do the job. Bear in mind that if you use keywords that nobody is looking for, your site will not receive visitors.

On the other hand, if you use the right keywords, you will still have to compete with similar sites to attract potential clients. Furthermore, your keywords will have to attract potential clients and not just people who want to have a look at your site out of curiosity.

It is suggested that every time that you are going to add something to your site (a title, an image, a text) you build a list with relevant words and use keywords tools to check their popularity and will suggest you words.

Ideally you should now have a list of relevant keywords that are being searched by your future customers. At the beginning, this activity could require a great deal of your time but, little by little, you will acquire more experience in SEO and this task will be faster and easier to fulfill.

A good idea to optimize your site is visiting the top-ten sites related to your niche and analyze their content, keywords, and its location within the texts, as well as, the links used in those sites.

Also, get some design ideas like colors, testimonials, and features on the sites. You might pick up some good proposals to improve the look and feel of your own website. Copy the success but being careful of not committing plagiarism.

It is important to upload the new page every time you make a modification, as it will attract search engine to new content. Even so, it is a good practice to check your ranking monthly as search engines change their algorithms often.

When you are ready to check your page rank, you can do it for FREE with the Google PageRank Report and focus your efforts on improving your result in the search engines.

Long Tail Keywords

Long Tail Keywords are sentences composed of three or more words that become a very specific search phrase used by consumers to find products or services that they wish to purchase.

When users want to find information or test the waters, they will usually introduce a single word or two words in the search engine.

Nevertheless, when they are ready to buy their search is more specific and they introduce more words trying to find exactly what they want. These words are known as long tail keywords.

If you want to attract customers to your site, just follow the same methods of your customers, but be careful do not become obsessed with SEO optimization and forget that your main task is Internet marketing.

Chapter 6: Link Building for Success

It is possible to generate a great amount of traffic through the use of hyperlinks and back-links from and to a website.

The hyperlinks are links inserted in any text, comment, image, or multimedia material that you upload to your website and should be directed to pages of prestige like academic institutions or powerful websites with similar content to yours. This allows Google to boost the position of your site, which will help you to improve the ranking and attract more traffic, boosting the popularity and quality of your site.

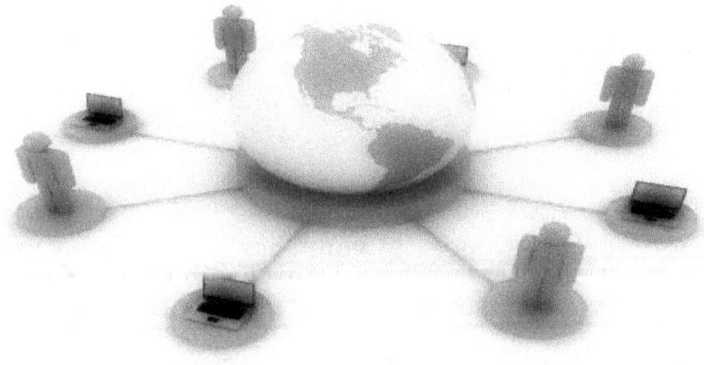

The blog WordPress offers you this option in its text section, although you can also easily create a link to the Word document using the link tool provided by WordPress.

The backlinks are links that generate traffic from and to your website. When you insert links to other sites in your website, you could build a special section like "Other Pages of Interest".

And remember to always choose quality over quantity, as Google is more interested in "quality" backlinks. Also, add links related to your website or the search engine will just ignore them and try to not manipulate links too much or Google will detect you and pull you out of the ranking.

Link Exchange

To obtain more links to your site you could reach an agreement with other sites to take on board reciprocal link exchanges, which is free of charge. Just bear in mind that those links must have quality and be related to your site.

You will have to learn to check out your link partners and avoid those with pages full of unrelated links that Google labels as "Bad Neighborhoods" or Google will devalue your website and drop it in the rank.

Therefore, avoid link exchanges with pages that take on board some or all of these practices:

- Black-hat techniques to drive traffic.
- Include numerous pages in outbound links.
- Do not include content but thousands of bad quality links just to try attracting traffic.
- Link farm and spam techniques: interlinked pages designed to confuse search engines and alter rankings making Google believe that the content of that site is more interesting than it actually is. Google has developed algorithms to detect and penalize these pages.

To decide whether a page is interesting or not, you have to pay attention to its activity, reputation, and number of visitors/followers.

To facilitate you with this task, there are some software programs and online tools that are able to help you check the quality and nature of those pages related to your website.

Play the game of reciprocity and if a site has links to your website, consider including a link to reciprocate, always make sure that the site is not a "bad neighbor". Otherwise, the other site will cut the links to your site, reducing your traffic and page rank. There are software programs and online tools that will help you check what sites you are linked to.

When creating links to and from your website, you must study your potential clients and focus your link efforts on attracting that audience to your website.

A good idea is to build little by little a directory of sites whose field of specialization is related to your site. -Use the search engines to find the top and interesting sites on the field.

Contact the webmasters requiring a link exchange and do not feel disappointed if some of them decline your offer, as a few will accept it and that means a lot of traffic running to your site.

When contacting the webmaster, mention some of the parts of his site that you liked and how a link from you would benefit his site visitors, this will offer the impression that you are really interested and that you are familiar with their website, which will increase your chances of getting a link.

At the moment of offering your link, provide HTML code for your link to the person responsible for the other website so they can just copy and paste it on their link page and make sure your URL is correct.

When displaying a link on your website, remember to add a small description to each link you display as it distinguishes your website from a link farm.

If you receive an offer for a link, check the content of the site carefully, its professionalism, and that they provide a link back to your site. Otherwise, you will be compromising the quality of your site and its exposure. Another thing to check out is whether or not they have a link on their home page to their link pages and if that is not the case, decline the invitation, as Google will not detect the link page and it would be totally worthless to you.

A powerful way to get quality links to your website is to submit articles to webmasters who publish newsletters focused on your niche. Not only will they appreciate new content for their readers, but also you will provide yourself with an interesting backlink for the search engines and hundreds of potential clients.

Finally, when you give your link to another site or you want to promote a product/service, the best thing to do is to upload that link to a bookmarking site like www.bitly.com. This is a free service where you can open an account and add links to be stored. If you want to use your links in a site, just go to your account in www.bitly.com and copy it. Besides presenting a better appearance on other websites, your link will be automatically abbreviated (very useful in pages like Twitter) and visible to all search engines, as this service generates an alert for the search engines.

Chapter 7: Writing Articles

Writing articles and submitting them to article directories is simple, but very powerful and effective way to create interest and generate traffic to your site and, it is FREE. Some of the most successful online marketers submit articles in order to attract attention to their products or services.

Through article directories, you submit an interesting and original article that people could use for free on their websites or blogs.

In exchange, they are required to display your name and website, including a link to your product/service/website, while leaving the content unchanged.

You may think that you are doing the job for others but actually, a single article of yours could be on display on several blocks so, you could attract more readers who, if feeling interested in your article, will link to your website.

When submitting an article to a directory, you should keep a number of aspects in mind:

- Use original and fresh content. You can create the content yourself but if you think that you do not have enough time or talent to write an article from scratch, you can always use PLR (Private Label Rights) content. Just decide what you want to write about and search for the issue on Google adding the words PLR.

For instance, if you have decided to write about weight loss introduce in Google, weight loss PLR. - PLR content can be free or paid content, it is varied and sometimes you could come across high quality e-books, reports, or articles. When using PLR, you will have to rewrite around 50% or 60% of the content to create an original article. This means, you could use the idea but changing the content or you will be committing a crime against intellectual property.

Do not try to use a PLR article, as it is very likely that other people have already used it and your article will be refused for being duplicated. Besides, when PLR content is not modified, it has to be shown as is, including the name and website link of the original author, which means that you will be generating traffic to the site of that author and not to your site.

- Read some articles in any directory on your niche topic and get ideas for new articles on the same subject.

Public domain repositories offer free material like software, books, music, designs, photographs, etc., which are very useful at the moment of creating an innovative article. Just search for public domain through Google.

- Elaborate articles related to the services or products that you are promoting on your website. In this way, you will attract to your web, people who are interested in that particular niche and, therefore, the chances of obtaining potential clients will increase.

- The articles should be around 300-500 words in length and be keyword-optimized.

- The articles should be interesting and linked to your products or services, offering information and providing solutions, but avoiding turning them into mere promotion letters or they will not be published.

- If you are selling a book or e-book, for instance, write an article related to the issue exposed in your e-book, informing people and offering solutions while adding a sentence like "if you need more information, find a book on the subject in the next link: your website or link of your product".

- The browsing public is starving for information on any topic imaginable. You can find out what they are looking for in your niche by using any keyword generator. A good plan is to offer new solutions to old problems we all share like a how to remove a stain on your child's clothes or how to fix a stuck drawer.

- Be creative and your articles will be appearing all over the Internet. If you have a humorous story about how you discovered the solution, add it to the article.

- The most successful titles are those that include a number ("How to Lose Weight in 4 Weeks"), offer a solution ("How To...") or resolve a mystery ("The Secrets of...").

- Create a new list of steps to get something done, as people love handholding and step-by-step lists of techniques or processes to make their life easier.

- Remember that every article directory has different submission guidelines that have to be followed or your article will not get published.

- You can hire an articles submission service, which for a fee will submit your articles to hundreds of directories. Yet, they will not bear in mind the submission guidelines for each directory, so you could get refused in some of them.

- Some popular article directories are: www.ezinearticles.com, www.articledashboard.com, and www.articlemarketer.com.

Chapter 8: Newsletters & Ezines

Hundreds of webmasters publish niche newsletters or ezines (abbreviation of electronic magazine) weekly or monthly, as they work as a powerful traffic getter being the most effective way of attracting traffic for free.

A newsletter can contain links back to your website to help self-promotion and "refresh" people's memories that your site is still present and ready to deliver good content and products. Additionally, the newsletter can also contain teasers that will incite its readers to come to your website.

If you keep submitting newsletters to your subscribers and articles to directories, you will soon be considered an expert and an authority in the field which will be translated into more traffic to your website.

Before you start writing, analyze your audience to know who they are, what they are looking for, what problems do they need solutions for, and what niche and hobbies they are interested in.

To find out what your potential clients are looking for, pay particular attention to the comments made by in the articles as, on many occasions, they are looking for a solution to a problem and you could provide that solution.

Do not forget about fellow online marketers. Any serious marketer is always on the lookout for ways to improve his business and to make his life as a marketer easy and cost effective. If you have something that will reduce his workload, save him money, or result in more sales, what you have in your hands is actually worth more than the gold he is seeking.

With that information, you can directly address the problems and passions of the newsletter's membership and increase the value of your article submissions to the Webmaster while building a database of potential clients.

Remember that writing on the Internet is different than writing for any other medium or task. Newsletter and ezine subscribers want to feel like they belong to a community and are not just an email address, so keep your articles informal and friendly using plain English and bullet points or steps to explain facts.

One effective way to get free newsletter publicity is to take one of those problems that needed a solution and elaborate a small report, which will be offered as a bonus to the Webmaster. Webmasters are very interested in free bonuses for their subscribers and would welcome your offer as it increases subscriber loyalty. In exchange, you will gain huge exposure as your name and a link to your website will be included in the report.

By keeping your reputation active you will grow and Webmasters will show interest for your website and, very possible, add a link to your site on theirs in a visible location as you have become an authority in your niche. This means that your traffic will increase dramatically alongside your page rank.

On the topic of ezines, although effective in attracting traffic to your website, they are quite expensive and recent statistics have shown how only 8 out of 100 people who read an ezine will be willing to buy a product or service from that website. Therefore, some good advice is to stick to newsletters when the intention is generating traffic, as they are free and shorter while equally effective but bearing in mind that writing reports and article is not the main task, attracting traffic is.

Chapter 9: Forums

Join a forum focused on how to set an online business, make money from home, or a subject related to your site as a way of attracting traffic.

Although some forums are fee-based but most of them are free of charge and they have actually better results as the members have the same questions and problems and they will be willing to pay for the solution. Also, the free forums count with more members, so more chances of reaching a higher number of potential clients.

After introducing yourself as a new member with a brief and friendly post in the category set for the occasion, create a signature that appears at the end of every post you make and on any email or private message you may send. The signature may include your name and the link to your site and may be one or two brief sentences. A carefully constructed signature is viral and will zip around the Web.

Read the rules of the forum and find out how it works and its categories while knowing the moderators and what the most popular members write about. The next step will be to get active and participate in the forum asking questions and offering solutions.

Offer links to free resources or offer your own products for free (a report, an e-book, etc.) and win the trust of other members little by little. In doing so, you are building reputation within the forum, which is essential to go through the next step: initiate the marketing of your website.

If you just join a forum and try to self-promote straight away, nobody will buy your products or services because members of the forum do not know you and trust you. Besides, it is more than probable that you will be "invited" to leave the forum.

To succeed in a forum, you have to build a reputation as an expert before offering your products and services subtly.

Instead of selling directly, just offer a solution and then add a sentence like "if you need more information, visit this website: name of your website".

You can also consider the possibility of creating a discussion board or a forum on your own website to boost interactivity among your visitors. Visitors who have had a good experience on your discussion board will return when they have a problem to solve or just for the social aspect of it.

Furthermore, if your visitors are satisfied with your product/service or content, you could encourage them to let others know about and forward your free articles or newsletter, which will include a link to your site. This provides additional exposure and it will increase your database of potential clients.

Chapter 10: Syndicate Your Business

Another free marketing tool is the "Really Simple Syndication" or RSS. This process is a kind of feedback that you produce on your website.

You can select part of your content and create a kind of diary that people registered to your website will receive in a similar way to a newsletter. The selected content, which could be anything from articles to promotions or updates passing from special events, is added to an RSS document and then registered with an RSS publisher or aggregate.

If you are technical enough, there are a number of software programs that will help you in your task. Otherwise, you always could hire the services of a freelancer who will do the job for you.

The key to success is to create useful, short content, bearing in mind your target audience, as RSS is an easy and free way of releasing news and press release.

At the moment of publishing choose the specific category to reach your intended audience and avoid categorizing yourself into a hole. If your content can be useful or interesting to different audiences, submit it to different aggregates under different categories.

The fastest and easiest way to syndicate your content is through WordPress. WordPress has a RSS widget that can add side or foot tools in a simple click, and then, automatically generate and upload a briefing of your content and comments left by your visitors.

Chapter 11: Press Releases

A press release can help generate increased awareness and provide avenues of immense professional distribution.

Until recently, press releases were thought of as being restricted to newspapers, radio, and TV news slots. Now there are several online news sites that receive millions of visitors on a daily basis like Google News and Yahoo News. In fact, half of the online visitors spend some time on a news site.

Wire services like Business Wire, PR Newswire, PRWeb, and Market Wire simplify the process of populating current news content into the most popular search engines.

When you include fresh content in your site, the traffic will increase dramatically.

There are very specific formats for writing press releases and, therefore, it is worth to carefully read the terms and conditions of each press release website.

Use eye catching titles and friendly content easy to read, bearing in mind that you must be patient and do not try to sale immediately. See examples of "how to publish a press release" and remember that one well-written press release could be read by thousands of future customers. Press releases can also use links to your content and instant updates that will reach your followers immediately.

Chapter 12: Social Bookmarking Sites

Another free tool to develop your online marketing are the social bookmarking sites. When you search in Google for social bookmarking sites you will have a return of around 500 sites, some of them general and some of them focused on a concrete niche and basically all of them receive millions of visitors on a monthly basis.

Social bookmarking marketing is a method of promoting your product, brand, or even yourself by making yourself and your business known across several social bookmarking sites. Though, you have to be patient, as although this technique is very effective, it requires certain time to boost.

On the positive side, the social bookmarking sites will grant you and your business with the necessary visibility that will allow turning visitors into buyers. It also involves the recommendations of other Internet users about a particular website.

Social bookmarking is a new way of organizing information and categorizing resources, making everything easier to access in the process. The person creating the bookmark must assign a tag or a group of tags to each link or resource.

Social bookmarking services show who created particular bookmarks and also give access to other bookmarks created by the same person. Users can therefore make social connections with other users interested in the same topic by following these tags. As a user you can also see how many people have used a particular tag and search amongst all the resources with the same tag.

Users who enjoy access to a particular social bookmarking site can view the bookmarks chronologically, by categories (tags), through a search engine, or just randomly.

In order to create your own collection of social bookmarks or be able to view others', you must register with the social bookmarking website. The site will allow you to store bookmarks, make tags, and decide upon which of your tags should be made public and which should be kept private.

You can access your favorite websites from any computer and even from your mobile phone!

The site leader in number of visitors is www.digg.com, having around 25 million unique visitors on a monthly basis. On digg users can view all the stories or links that their fellow users submit. If a story gets enough 'diggs' it gets promoted to the front page of the Digg website. If it doesn't get enough 'diggs' it remains in the 'digg all' area, where it will eventually be removed.

All the content on the Digg website is free and there are no editors, so the editing is done by all the users together. To join it, simply sign up for a Digg account at digg.com and take off from there.

Whenever you want to submit an article, video, or pod cast, just post it for people to see and it will show up immediately in the section called 'Upcoming Stories'.

The top social bookmarking are:

1. www.digg.com
2. www.technorati.com
3. www.delicious.com
4. www.stumbleupon.com
5. www.reddit.com
6. www.fark.com
7. www.slashdot.org

As when joining a forum, check the ones that result more interested to you bearing in mind their content and, after carefully read the requirements to open a profile, participate in the site getting involved in activities to build a reputation by submitting articles or your blog posts and get ready to receive comments.

Invite your friends to join and share and remember that search engines love sites that receive lots of inbound links. A good initiative is to offer freebies like e-books or reports to the large sites like digg.com or MySpace.com with links to your page, which will be visible and available to millions of users.

The fact of the matter is FREE information spreads across the Internet at the speed of light.

Here are some methods that you can employ to get the most benefit from social bookmarking:

• When you create a blog post, make sure that the keyword phrase is as close to the beginning of the post as possible. When you bookmark the post, use the title of the post and tag the keyword as well. This is great for search engine results.

• Social bookmarking leads to more people reading your articles, posts, etc. and over time this will create additional credibility for you. It can also lead to repeat traffic, referrals, sales, newsletter sign ups, comments on your blogs, emails from readers, etc.

• Stay active and interact on the social bookmarking website and bookmark every post.

• The content on your website must have quality over quantity.

Chapter 13: Create a Blog

Blogs are, undoubtedly, a great free traffic driving tool. Open your blog for free in sites like Blogger or WordPress and do not worry if you are not very technical, as WordPress does not require any technical or computing knowledge as everyone can set his/her own website just by following a few simple step described in the blog.

Additionally, WordPress has some good advantages like the fact that it is free of charge while it offers a great number of gidgets that are very easy to set and use and are able to transform your page into a highly professional website.

You can also create a blog within your website which will add a "human" touch to the site. Blogs also provide features that can generate traffic and exposure like pinging that allows for each update to the blog to be pinged and updated on blog directories which count with thousands and even millions followers.

Blogs are able to generate huge amounts of traffic because people like reading new content and if you enjoy writing and can put your personality across then a blog could be the best free traffic generator you ever have.

You do not need to write every single day as you always can "borrow" content from other sites like videos from YouTube, content from social networking platforms like Facebook or Twitter, or news from online newspapers.

Obviously, you should add links to your products and to affiliate marketing partners (explained in further chapters).

Commenting on Blogs

Find out blogs related to your field of specialization and check whether or not you can place comments on them, as commenting on blogs will grant you more exposure and the chance of building a reputation on the field. This is especially the case with content sites. When commenting on a blog, your website address is also shown to all the users of those blogs while your comments can work as product promotion. As always, remain brief and concise on comments and avoid direct sales.

Chapter 14: Ping Services

You can help the search engine find results by informing them every time you update your blog. You do this by sending a 'ping' to the major directories every time you add a new posting to your blog.

The technology behind the ping function is, nevertheless, not new or solely related to blogging. It is, in fact, a simple program that has been used for many years as a way of making sure that a certain IP address actually exists and is able to accept requests from remote machines.

Pings have become increasingly important to bloggers as a part of their efforts to keep search engines informed about their latest updates. Bloggers inform the various search engine and aggregation services such as social bookmarking websites by sending a ping to these service providers.

Once the service receives an appropriate ping signal from a website, it is taken as a confirmation that something has been updated on that blog or website.

The service then visits the blog or website in question and immediately indexes any new content it discovers.

Having the ability to actively 'ping' an update message to all of the major directories means that search engines no longer need to regularly visit blogs to discover new changes.

Pings allow bloggers to make the first move by informing search engines of changes when they happen. This allows search engines to be more efficient by reporting and showing updated links as soon as they happen. It also means that blogs are indexed on time.

For you, it means that new content on your website is presented to the public in a more timely fashion whether you rely on search engines or social bookmarking websites for your traffic. When you send a ping to the social bookmarking website where you are registered, it knows immediately that there is some interesting new material out there and puts it forth for their users to view.

Most of the blog authoring tools automatically ping a server every time you update an existing post or create a new one.

The blog authoring tool sends a signal to one or more ping servers. The ping server then creates a list of the blogs that have new, updated material. The best independent ping servers are www.pingomatic.com and www.kping.com, although if you use WordPress, this blog will save you work and, time as, it offers a plugin that will send a signal directly to the ping services every time you post content.

Chapter 15: Viral Marketing

One more option to increase your visibility is through viral marketing. To set up this option you have to offer an e-book or report with resale rights and include your affiliate links or even links to other websites you might be using.

You should clearly specify the e-book has resale rights only and, therefore, the content can be resold but not changed. In this way, your visitors will download your e-book because they are getting useful information for free and a product that they can resale on their own websites.

The marketing strategy lies in the fact that the content cannot be altered, which means that your affiliate links or website URLS will get exposed to many other people who visit their websites or buy the resale rights book, increasing the chances that you gain visitors and obtain sales or leads.

Chapter 16: Pay per Click (PPC)

Pay-per-click advertisements works by displaying a list of advertising on your site and giving you a commission when someone clicks on one of them.

This commission can range from as low as $0.01 to as high as $100 depending on the company, though most of the time you will earn just a few cents.

Usually, large insurance companies are the ones more willing to pay the best commission per click and you could get a decent amount if you manage to have a decent number of legitimate clicks (clicks from genuine visitors). Still, bear in mind that the search engines can detect when someone is doing irregular clicks and that is considered a fraud, which means that not only your affiliate program will be over but that you can also have serious legal problems.

As regards approval, you have to follow a similar process to the one required in affiliate marketing website, although pay-per-click sites are usually less strict and it is more than likely you received an approval.

You would show as many advertisements from other income streams as you want, always make sure that your website offers interesting content for the visitors.

Also you can add an ad through the pay-per-click method using the Google service Adwords. This service is not free but you can establish expense limits in your campaigns.

Another alternative is to pay every time that someone does click in one of your ads. This service works by fixing bids between $0.01 and a few thousand dollars. The higher your bid is, the higher Adwords will display your ad in the search engines.

There are cheaper services like www.bidvertiser.com that, although is not as powerful as Google Adwords, is most accessible concerning costs and you could include in your ads a higher number of keywords, which means that you could equal the traffic obtained through Google. Therefore, it is essential to use the keywords analysis tools to search for popular general sentences and words at the moment of fixing a bid.

One more thing to bear in mind is that a PPC ad is not recommended when you are starting your business and you cannot offer a star product/service or have a solid client database because you could actually lose a considerable amount of money and will not obtain visible results.

Chapter 17: Cost per Action Advertising

The so-called Cost per Action, (CPA) advertising is similar in appearance to pay-per-click ones. Like pay-per-click ads, they show themselves in the form of small text advertisements on the top, bottom, left, or right sides of the website. -The difference with pay-per-click advertising is that while the first only requires a click on them to grant a small commission, CPA advertisings must lead to a sale or other similar action.

At the moment, the best-known CPA networks are those related to Azoogle (search on Google) and these types of websites should be focused as a complement or alternative to pay-per-clicks.

A good piece of advice is to apply for the affiliate program of Azoogle only when you have a decent amount of traffic coming to your website, otherwise, you are more likely to be refused.

Chapter 18: Buying Publicity Space

Buying online publicity space is another way to make money while trying to attract more traffic to a website. You could find pages that offer publicity space like www.adbrite.com or even www.ebay.com.

An important factor to bear in mind at the moment of looking for a website to publish an ad, is to choose a site related to the ad to be published.

Also, you have to make sure that the website where you wish to include your ad enjoys a good position in the ranking of results of the search engines and that your own website already has enough content to be identified as interesting by the visitors.

Chapter 19: Incentive Marketing

The incentive marketing is a method of online advertising, being the most popular one the so-called "paid-to" pages, which are sites that pay their visitors for reading ads.

Although the cost of these campaigns are relatively low and visitors will actually have to read the ad in order to receive the payment, many Webmasters do not use incentive marketing, arguing that most visitors are only interested in making money and not in the ad or the product.

In other words, most of visitors will not buy the product or service promoted, they simply will read the ad and get paid for it. The only positive factor here is that this alternative is effective at the moment of generating traffic to your website.

Chapter 20: Buying Online Traffic

Buying traffic could be beneficial to increase the number of visitors in a spectacular manner. Yet, you will never be sure whether that traffic is real or your visitors are fake; and in this last case, your investment will be wasted.

If you decide to buy traffic, it is important to hire the service of a company that uses real domains that are not being used. In this way, the links will be real and you will have many more choices of generate real traffic to your website.

Chapter 21: Affiliate Marketing

Affiliate marketing is when you promote another company's website, service, or product in return for a commission, which is usually given when a sale or lead is actually made from your advertising methods. There is also the possibility of receiving commissions for click, this means that if the URL of a company received a click through an advertising placed on your website.

In both cases, the URL of the company contains a special coding that would trace back to your affiliate account and, therefore, they know when a sale or lead is received through your website or advertising.

Most of the major companies on the Internet, like www.amazon.com or www.bestby.com, are using affiliate marketing. However, they do not necessarily advertise their affiliate opportunities blatantly and most time you have to search for the option "Affiliate Program" on their websites or send a message presenting your application to become an affiliate.

In general terms, the company will require some general information like your name, address, telephone number, and website. -Once your application is submitted, you have to wait for a few days for approval.

Another way of joining an affiliate program is through an affiliate network where, after being granted with their approval, you could apply for more than one company at the same time. Once your application is approved, you get access to an account manager where you can start applying for the affiliate programs of specific companies.

One of the most popular affiliate networks is www.commissionjunction.com. To start working with them, you need the approval of a URL, which you can get through a web hosting company or a domain name service and sign up in the section "Publishers".

Once you are approved, the site will let you know what companies you want to work for while showing a list of the companies organized by category. -But, you will need a significant amount of funds upfront to be able to pay affiliates.

Another very popular network site is www.clickbank.com. Signing up with www.clickbank.com is very easy as a URL is not required and the approval process is done instantly.

Nevertheless, it is not as large as Commission Junction, but is has the advantages that you do not need funds upfront to get involved in the affiliate program nor need technical expertise, as the site takes care of everything.

Chapter 22: Social Networking

Participate in Social Networking Platforms. Find networks for general purposes and those related to your industry and register with them. Use your profile to introduce your site and products or services and, if the platform allows you to do so, place a link to your website on your profile page.

The most popular social networking sites for general content is Facebook, which boasts high levels of activity and membership and, therefore, a great opportunity to increase your contact base.

You can increase traffic by commenting on walls and create applications and widgets that the network can support. Facebook also offers a chance to build your traffic for a reasonable price.

The other important social networking site is Twitter. The difference with Facebook is that you could set your account in such a way that anyone can visit and join your profile, which is great if what you are looking for is exposure.

You can open an account for your business or each product or service that you wish to promote, as there is not limit in the number of profiles that you could open.

Participation is paramount at this platform. So, ask and answer questions and promote content, products, and services to generate Twitter.

Do not forget to use your signature and link to your site. Visit other people's account, reply, and return visits and comments for those who came by yours to boost presence in the site.

Chapter 23: Mailing Lists

E-mailing list is a cheap and effective way of keeping in touch with your clients and offering them an incentive to come back. Emails can be easily personalized thanks to software programs and are very low-maintenance.

The key here is to build a strong database of clients and future potential clients. You can do this through jumping into a joint adventure with another Webmaster who targets the same niche as you, but in a different capacity and ask him/her to promote each other to your clients. In this way, the database of both websites will increase with the clients of both sites. The faster way of building a database is to offer something for free. This could be a report, webinar, software program, e-book, etc. and ask visitors to introduce their name and email address to get the freebie. You can also ask fellow Webmasters and bloggers to offer the free item to their clients.

Another option is to find Facebook and Twitter accounts specialized in the field of your e-book or report and ask them to offer the freebie to their followers.

In this way, you will increase your database while generating huge traffic to your website.

One more alternative to build a client database is to join a Joint Adventure, which consists in exchanging promotional campaigns with the responsible person for other websites in your same sector, but which offer different products or services. In this way, the responsible party for the other page will offer your products/services to his/her clients and you will offer his/her services/products to your clients. Eventually, both pages will benefit from each other's database of clients.

While you build your client database, think about the possibility of using a marketing service through emails like www.ConstantContact.com, which will help you send emails that include surveys, which will offer you a global vision about the products or services in which your potential clients are interested.

Chapter 24: Off-line Marketing

Although off-line marketing could be seen as very traditional and out of fashion, it is actually still effective. There are several methods to attract visitors through off-line marketing:

- Direct mail. Consists of sending advertisements through mailings like postcards, flyers, or brochures. The negative to this is the cost of this strategy, considering that you will have to get stamps, envelopes, and paper, plus paying the bill of the post office. On the positive side, through mailing you could build a long lasting "relationship" with your future customers, as many people will not buy from mailings, but if they like your site enough they may bookmark it and decide to buy later.

- Free Bulletin Board Advertising. Many supermarkets, fast food restaurants, and department stores offer community advertising on bulletin boards.

Most of the time these advertising spaces are free and, although you probably will not get hundreds of customers, you will not lose anything.

- Print Media. This is the most classical advertising method of all. They are affordable and, believe it or not, they are still very successful at reaching future potential customers.

- Phone Book. If you budget allows you to do so, you should consider the possibility of placing an ad in your local phone book including, of course, your website address.

- Do not forget to carry your business cards on you at all times, so you could promote your website at every social event.

Chapter 25: Other Ways of Generating Traffic

There are two types of traffic, natural and organic traffic. Natural traffic is the traffic that can come naturally to the site mainly through the name and the keyword content of the site. The domain name of the site plays a big part in the game as a well-chosen domain name, which is immediately associated to the product or content offered, basically guarantees a visit to the website.

On the other side, the term organic traffic refers to the traffic that is 'sent' to the site through the well use of SEO techniques.

The search engines have software programs called crawlers, or spiders, which search the sites looking for keywords and tags to build a list of search-related features to generate the ranking page. Therefore, the optimization of keywords is crucial to be picked up by the crawlers. Bear in mind that around 10% of the traffic diverted to the site is obtained thanks to the keywords.

Also, the more information available for a page, the easier it is for those programs to reference the page. This means that each page contains in your website should include a title and headers with powerful keywords.

Your best bet would also be to include the most relevant information of the site in the first paragraph of the home page. The search engines usually search in the first 2-3 lines of the first paragraph to compile results.

Finally, you should know that crawlers avoid picking poor links or under construction pages on the site and, therefore, regular maintenance and updates of links and pages contribute to keeping your site in a high position within the ranking.

Other methods to generate organic traffic are:

- Submit the site to directories and other guides on the Internet, as they will give your site more exposure in the search engines. Listing with directories that target the same field of expertise that your website can also enhance its placement on the web and attract new potential clients.
- Create internal links to increase the chances of navigating within the website, which could be very useful to content sites.

- Provide the geographical location of the business – this works mostly for product-based sites, as the likelihood of someone choosing to buy something in their area is enhanced.

- Listing products/content topic individually – the more pages on the site, the more a site is considered 'worthy' of being included in search engine results.

Specific pages for specific content also show in-depth knowledge about the product/content, enhancing the reputation of the site as a good destination.

- Buy Banner Ads. Buying banner ads (which is an advertisement) on other sites provides exposure as they include a link to the site promoted. A banner is just an advertisement but more eye-catching for visitors who will remember banners easily.

You can also join a banner exchange program in order to increase visibility on the web. The banner exchange program works on a swap ratio of 2:1 usually, this means that for every 50 views on your website, in return your banner will be posted on 25 other websites.

- Buy text links to boost the possibilities of being picked up by search engines.

- Use Tag Images. Tags are an important aspect of search engine optimization and search engines set photos high in ranking so remember to tag your images to gain exposure and attract the search engines.

Adding tags to pictures allow for photo searches to generate the photo and the address of the site. This works especially well for sites that sell products, as a tag placed on your product pictures help to attract people to your website when an image search is set.

- Hosting Regular Promotions. Sales and discount are two words that work wanders for attracting people to the website.

- Update Content on a Regular Basis. If visitors see the same information again and again on your website, it is very probable that they will never return. Updating content on a regular basis will keep visitors coming back as fresh content is found.

Besides, search engines are constantly looking for new content and they keep the site on a high position. Furthermore, when it comes down to content-base sites, updated content means more pages and more viewers, which is its aim in increasing traffic. You do not have to write large articles every day, just include regular briefings, images, videos, news, etc.

- Get Reviews. Require top sites on your sector to provide reviews on your site to build visibility. However, bear in mind that this applies when the reviews are good.

- Offer Freebies. Giving away freebies is another way of generating additional traffic to a site. Offering a freebie for every purchase will increase your sales considerably, while retaining your buyers who will not doubt to buy more products or services from you in a future. You can offer a great variety of stuff as freebie, especially when it comes down to content-base sites.

These freebies can consist of templates for specific document, e-books, reports, classes or seminars, webinars, a dictionary of terms of the industry/niche, checklists for a task, a live advice chat room, free consulting, etc.

- Include Additional Resources. An option for content sites is to feature an additional resources section, which will display links to other websites. In return, the websites on the list can mention that they are suggested by your site or/and include a link to your own site. Also, products-base websites can include links to related items or guides such as maintenance for the product they offer.

Remember to reply to queries and comments as it will enhance your site and offer a nice experience to your visitors. People do not like to be ignored and by answering questions and comments visitors will feel the "human" side of your website, as robotic content is a deterrent for many Internet users.

For a content site, it shows that you are dedicated to providing information accurately and for a product or service website, it may show customer support and willingness to take care of the clients.

- Hold Contests and Promos. People generally love to play and win. In either case, a person who took part in the contest will come back to check the results.

- Have Your Own Domain. This builds brand recognition and easy association of your content/product in viewers' minds. The name can even become a brand in the long run.

- Offer Free Consulting. In this way, you will establish yourself as an expert on your field while attracting people to visit and participate on your website. Regarding to product-base sites, samples and trial runs or demonstrations of products work in the same way of free consulting.

- Ensure Accessibility. A site that is easily accessible, easy to navigate and browse, and does not hurt the eyes, encourages more people to visit it than sites which are complicated and cluttered.

- Offer Uniqueness. Give your visitors a unique experience and content and atmosphere to boost the chances that they decide to come back.

- Provide Follow-Up. Especially useful for product-based sites. Following up with clients will create a good impression of your site and give the clients the feeling that they are dealing with a professional. Auto mail and responders also work, and can be used by content sites.

- Create Exit Pop-ups. The pop-ups work in such a way that when a visitor abandons your website, a window pops up and he or she will be taken to another address.

You can use an exit popup program where you can register your website and as a window pops up from exiting your site, your site can pop up the same way on another website that is taking part in the program. In this way, clients who may not know of your site can be exposed to it in this way.

- Joint Ventures. Participating in joint ventures will help you to boost your visibility in the Net. Joint ventures can be focused on links exchange, banner swaps, referrals, and reviews.

Chapter 26: Check Results

Some pages allow you to check the results of your website, giving you information about your products and services, including how many visitors your site receives or how much traffic (and from where) is generated to your website. This is a task that you will need to take on board to know what campaigns/services/products are working and which are not producing the expected results.

The most popular of these pages is www.visitorville.com that shows results in the form of video games in exchange for a monthly fee that will directly depend on the number of visitors received in your website.

Another very popular site is www.statcount.com, that shows information through statistics using classical graphs and anagrams but it is cheaper than www.visitorville.com and free in the case your website does not get more than 270,000 visits per month.

Although both pages will offer you information about where your traffic is coming from, www.statcount.com also informs you about those keywords which are more searched by visitors.

Chapter 27: Conclusion

The World Wide Web has dramatically grown over the last years and, right now, anything and everything that you could imagine or look for is just a click away. In fact, many people can no longer imagine a life without Internet access while any business that is serious about its future has a presence on the Internet.

The internet is vast and intricate, and offers users more choice as they can choose what site they wish to visit or compare different products and services before buying, saving a great deal of time and having a large variety to choose from.

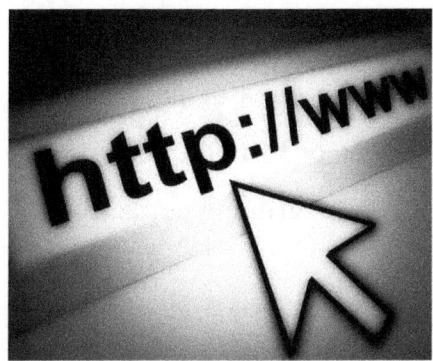

The Internet is the most vibrant commercial market place in the world. The place where almost everyone goes to buy, sell, bargain, promote, publicize, and advertise and yet, at the moment we are merely scratching the surface, and the ultimate possibilities that the web may be able to offer us are essentially endless.

Differently from a physical business, which could be visited by people walking by, an online business can be visited by anyone, everywhere in the world and the entire world is your potential market.

The potential of Internet marketing is infinite and right now thousands of people have been able to earn enough money through some type of online business to quit their full-time jobs.

It is not unusual to come across testimonies of people who are making real fortunes online; you only need initiative, innovation, and hard work to make your dreams come true.

While the possibilities are endless, you have to compete with many other online businesses, which offer products or services similar to yours.

Therefore, you need to find out strategies to take advantage of the power of the Internet and market your product much more efficiently. There are millions of websites in the Net competing for clients' attention and you have to make an effort in order to grab your share.

You must also remember that any business needs some investment to take off. So, be prepared to spend some money in your business and be willing to invest in your own success! The good news is that an online business requires far less investment than a physical one and that your business will certainly pay off all the money that you will invest.

When stepping into online marketing, you will see how you will acquire knowledge little by little passing from learning how to build a basic website to attracting traffic and registering on affiliate programs passing for struggling to write a decent sales letter.

With the pass of the months, you will learn that the key of your success lies on the traffic that you will be able to generate to your website or products and to what extent you will manage to reach and keep clients or potential clients.

In order to succeed, any business needs to receive visitors. On the subject of online businesses, if you wish for your business to flourish, you must find ways to constantly sustain and increase your traffic flow using the strategies outlined in this book that will help you to fulfill your task.

By now, you have learned to develop a website; to attract potential clients; to increase the flow of your online traffic; and to develop some online marketing techniques.

Now you only have to use all this information and strategies to reach your goals!

Say hello to the new marketer in you and enjoy the experience!

Index of Illustrations

1. Internet at Home. Author: jb2.0/www.flickr.com.
2. HTML. Author: SEOPlanter/www.flickr.com
3. I Love Internet. Author: Codiceinternet/flickr.
4. WWW. Author: SEOPlanter/www.flickr.com
5. Google Search. Author: Telendro/www.flickr.com.
6. SEO Words. Author: SEOPlanter/www.flickr.com
7. Marketing Online. Author: FindYourSearch www.flickr.com.
8. The Internet. Author: Colombia Ministry of New Technology/ www.flickr.com.
9. Profits. Author: Por 401(k)20123/www.flickr.com
10. Blog. Author: ZERGE_VIOLATOR/www.flickr.com
11. Ping Symbol. Author: jb2.0/www.flickr.com.
12. Facebook Logo. Author: Marcopako/www.flickr.com.
13. Online Traffic. Author: esocialmediashop/flickr.com
14. Searching. Author: Rock1997/www.commonswikipedia.org

www.ingramcontent.com/pod-product-compliance
Lightning Source LLC
Chambersburg PA
CBHW051735170526
45167CB00002B/949